A Journey of Life's Lessons

Short Stories in Poetic Form of Inspiration and Self-Reflection

by

C. L. Givens

Cork Hill Press
Carmel

Cork Hill Press
597 Industrial Drive, Suite 110
Carmel, IN 46032-4207
1-866-688-BOOK
www.corkhillpress.com

Trade Paperback Edition: 1-59408-275-8

Printed in the United States of America

1 3 5 7 9 10 8 6 4 2

Dedications

To my children (the 2 J's) Jabari and Jamiya; you are my love, my life and my inspiration. Always strive to be individuals no matter what others may think or say.
Love Ya!

I especially appreciate the patients and attention of loved ones that listened to me whenever God placed ideas into my spirit. LaNell Williams (you have been my number one cheerleader.) Dawn Givens and Shonnette Givens, thanks for listening, especially in the times you weren't in the mood. (You acted the part.) Thank you André McKinney for your insight and for being my consultant from a male's perspective.

Special Thanks to my friend, LaShunda Williams who always took time out to listen to my thoughts and rough drafts anytime (Day or night). I would also like to thank my Sister Kanita and Brother Gary and their families. And to the family and friends that would come out and support me during "Pass The Mic" nights @ Sankofa Arts Kafe. To all of the people I have come in contact with in my lifetime, you all played a part in my "journey of life's lessons". A special thanks to Pastor Rickie G. Rush for his leadership and teachings. Be Blessed!

Book Contents

LIFE (Inspiration)

LOVE (Reflection)

ETERNITY (Final Destination)

LIFE
(Inspiration)

Introduction to the Journey: The Journey Begins

Alpha and Omega, the cause of the wind
The calm in the storm when it seems that
On this journey I've sometimes walked alone
I know you'll be with me until the end.
The Ultimate friend, like no other friend.

When no words can be spoken,
The rhythm and flow of my pen and pad
Giving me the right things to say
You are the brush across my face
I awaken to everyday.

The excitement of ideas you place in my spirit
Overwhelms me like nothing else.
When I have no one to listen or share my joy with
I've learned to encourage myself.

In knowing where these words are coming from,
But not knowing who they pertain to,
I think back to a time I ask you
To" use me like you wanted me to be used."

Say what people were going through,
Words that many were afraid to face or speak out loud.
There's comfort in knowing that I'm making you proud.

I'm willing to follow where you lead
Even when people in my life begin to leave.
My journey is not their journey
This path I'll take is my own
As long as I know your hedge of protection is around me,
This trip, I'm willing to travel alone.

In reading this, if it only inspires two or three,
I'm O.K. with that because it keeps on blessing me.

Silent Sadness

I sit and listen to the birds sing
They are without a care in the world.
While I'm trying to figure out
How these bills are getting paid,
And needing to buy new shoes for my baby girl.

As the world turns, and as this candle burns
That now is my source of light.
Cause I haven't worked in about six months,
And my Electricity got turned off last night!

I have been searching for work though
But there are some things I refuse to do.
For some I've been overqualified, or underqualified
Or my skin was not quite the right hue.

And in my silent struggle,
[I've got my pride]
And don't want to admit to anyone
How I'm about to loose my place.
I'd rather keep this wall up,
Hide behind my smile, and continue making it on grace.
Not wanting to hear later on about
"All you've done for me"
Thrown up in my face.

Or I figure I'll depend on state assistance for a little while.
Not because I really want to, but for the well being of my child.

My prayer is that I make it through this trial,
And never to be in this kind of situation again.
This silent depression has taken its toll on me
And my hair is falling out daily in big strands.

TO TOP IT ALL OFF!
Taking pieces of my spirit with him,
My husband just left me.
Leaving me lost and bewildered
With my soul feeling empty.

I CAN'T TAKE MUCH MORE OF THIS!
(LORD, LORD WHAT AM I TO DO!)?
I Know-
Tonight when I lay down to rest,
I'll pray that in eternal sleep I'll go.
Hold'n on to childhood secrets
Disappointments, and failures in life,
Going out this way
No one will ever know.

Cause (I've got my pride)
So I'll suffer in silence
Though people would not have known the real me.
I wish at times
I could be like the birds
(Not having a care in the world)
And fly away beyond the trees.

Who Has My Back? (Inspiration in Seven Lines) And The Answer in Five Letters

If I'm the one everyone turns to,
Where do I turn when I'm going through?

Going through the trials and storms of life that we all may face.
Who will step in and take my place?

If I'm the counselor for everyone else's issues,
Who will counsel me when I need someone to turn to?

JESUS!!

Life's Lessons

You can't always blame the devil for all of what you go
through
It just maybe God allowing things to happen to you.

You must keep the faith and stand strong,
When the storms of life seem to be lasting long.

God has his own timetable
When it may appear to you
That you've been struggling
For far too many days.
Trust in his word,
And know that trouble really doesn't last always.

It's true when they say,
He won't ever leave or forsake you.
This I know from personal experiences to be true.

Trying your best to do all YOU think you should
While hearing the choir sing,
"Oh Taste and See That The Lord is Good."

Right then you think,
That this couldn't apply to the situation you're going
through.
Unless you have had an intimate encounter with him,
These are just words to you.

But not until, your body is healed,
When the doctor says he's done all he can do.
The songs sung, stories heard,
And those words in the Bible start meaning something to you.

You'll then become to understand
That everything you've ever gone through,
Was a part of His plan.

He wants to know if you'll be able to be trusted with a blessing
And if you have been taking heed of your
Life's Lessons.

Just because it may look as though your prayer requests
Haven't come to pass
You must have faith to know that
God is moving things in your path.

He's working it out in the spirit realm.
When the manifestation does occur,
It will be so unexplainable that you'll know
It was no one else but
HIM!

Poem Delivery

I want you to hear these words, feel these words,
So that after I've spoken and you leave,
My words resonate in your spirit
And become etched in a part of your memory.

Thinking to yourself:
Someone out there has actually given your story a voice in a way;
When you where too ashamed to talk about your own mess,
Or just didn't know what to say.

I want to be able to deliver this message to you and you believe,
Whether true or not,
That each one of these stories are personally about me.

Putting these words in your mind so you can see,
That no matter what your situation is,
You can still be what you want to be.

Have faith in God so you'll know,
Everything you've experienced in life
Is supposed to help you grow.

In life, I've been through highs, lows, heartaches and pain,
So my journalizing them has become a therapeutic tool I use.
I want you to hear these words, feel these words,
Even if the subject matter does not pertain to you.

Just for one moment step outside of your issues,
To mentally walk in someone else's shoes.

Diversity of Poetry

Poetry represents serenity for me.
Being able to record deep rooted feelings and thoughts allow me to be free.
Taking me to places unknown and exploring depths of imagery.

While others make analyzing your words harder than what it needs to be.
What may hold healing and meaning for you may not make sense to me.
But that's the uniqueness of this art, and recognizing your creativity.
Don't discredit a writer's work simply because you don't understand what they were trying to say or do.
Open your mind to consider that their subject matter may not be directed towards you.

Respect the diversity in the poetry game.
Every style of poetry is not the same.

Poetry does not have to rhythm,
In every second or third line.

Poetry is a free-style art so "whatever will be will be."
Poetry "is what it is", even if yours doesn't make sense to me.

To The Critics

What Is Family?

Is it a mother and father,
With two kids, and a dog, living in a big house,
With a white picket fence outside?
Every morning mom seeing dad off to work, kids to school,
As she's left to take care of all of the chores inside.

Making her feel as if home is her only place.
Because chores have to be done, Dinner prepared
And at the end of the day when everyone returns,
She still has to wear her game face.

-MAYBE-

Maybe it's the father
Getting his hustle on at the end of the street.
So the children he desperately loves
Can keep a roof over their heads and shoes on their feet.

-WHO'S TO SAY-

Could it be the mother without any outside help
Working her fingers to the bones just to make her ends come together?
Putting her faith in God
When she really wants to break down ad cry,
But deep inside,
She knows her struggles won't last forever.

Or is the grandmother
Who's raising your kids for you?
Not even considering the fact that
She may have dreams that she would like to pursue.

As for me;
It was three girls and a loving
(Yet strict) mother,
Were in the family I grew up with.
Looking back now,
Some of my personal choices I may have changed,
But for THAT family I wouldn't trade it!

Cause God knows,
Had it not been for that Mother staying on me,
I would not have become the woman
I have grown to be.

I've said all of this to say;

It doesn't matter who you share your household with,
Whether there's a bunch of y'all,
Or maybe just a few.
The meaning of that word FAMILY
May be defined differently to each and every one of you.

So don't let another special occasion go by,
A Family reunion, Funeral or Holiday,
To express love for your family
Because that time is TODAY.

When I Grow Up

I've heard it said before that
You should give people their flowers while they're alive.
Well in giving these flowers I take much pride.
Because this particular woman is quite alive.

Matter of fact
It's hard to catch her at home.
When you call her,
Expect to get the answering machine, because she's always gone.

A woman of her caliber exemplifies a picture of health.
Substitute teaching, riding horses, and if you let her,
She'll turn a flip!

Active in her church and her community,
With snow cones being sold in her yard under her shade tree.

Easter egg hunts being held at her house,
With numerous dogs running in and out.

Taking care of people is what she likes to do.
Always seeming to have a positive attitude.

Or maybe I catch her on the right day,
Never hearing her have a negative word to say.

Oh, and I can't forget to include
How at the family parties, you better step aside.
Because when the music plays
She's running to the dance floor to do the
ELECTRIC SLIDE.

One fact I can't exclude, because it is a must.
The woman I've just described is 70 plus.

That's the type of role model I like to see.
When I grow up,
She's the kind of woman I strive to be.

Single By Choice, or Are Bad Choices Keeping Me Single?

The majority of women in my family are single.
And this is something that I don't desire for me.
Besides, I do plan on being married
Before I turn forty.

Is it that they have had to be too independent?
Or are the issues they have too deep
For a man to contend with?

-I Don't Know-

Is it that they can't submit or compromise?
Or do they tend to fall in love
With the wrong type of guys?

After all, you just can't submit to any average Joe.
How will you take instructions from someone that
Doesn't know anymore than you know?

That's like the blind leading the blind.
In order for submission to occur,
The mate of my choosing has to have a renewed mind.

I don't believe being alone was God's intent.
I'm trying my best to keep the faith
And hold out for my Prince.

On the other hand,
I have a male cousin who's following the same path.
Every time we get together
(About the subject) we share good laughs.

After College, he became a coach
(Still being a single man)
Now residing in Austin and doing the best he can.

My thinking is that he has unreal expectations
Of his helpmate.
But then again who am I to say,
He knows better than I do about the woman he'd like to date.

I feel he's such a genuine
(Although anal guy), who has a lot of love to share.
I hope we both find that ONE
Before we grow too old to care.

The rate time is passing by,
Before we are aware
We'll be back at grandmamma's house
Sitting up laughing in that blue rocking chair.

Change of Plans

I had everything mapped out for myself
After high school;
The goals I set, and the way my life would be.
Calling my own shots, living single and free with limited responsibilities.

To find a permanent suitor was later in the plan;
Because I always said,
I wouldn't have kids without a husband.

Until, my life took a different direction,
Not yet married, but not single anymore,
I had a son at 22
And a daughter at 24.
The picture I drew of my fairy tale life, soon flew out the door.

Now it's just Me, my Prince and Princess
Known to me as the two J's.
They are my strength that gets me through tough days.

Even though in appearance they resemble,
They have different interest, like most siblings do.
One likes reading, while the other likes playing Play Station II.

That girl of mine likes to study a bunch,
While the boy is always looking forward to lunch.

Praying together is what we like to do;
Never forgetting to give God thanks
For all he's brought us through.

Though my life didn't go the direction I had in mind,
The way things turned out with us is fine.

I know I'm truly blessed,
Because I thought God couldn't straighten out this mess.

Although conceived out of wedlock,
I Thank God for the kids I got!

C. L. Givens

Can't We All Just Get Along?

Why, as a race can't we uplift and encourage each other,
Instead of like crawfish
Pulling each other back down into the pot.
In fear that one of us may obtain something that the other hasn't got.

Other races can live together in a household
And help each other
Without being jealous of their success.
While some of us try keeping up with the Joneses;
Or finding others to impress.

Black people especially; we have jealousy in our race.
Seeing another Sista and tearing her down
(Non-verbally)
Right in her face.

The women will prejudge another at first glance;
Without even giving her a fair chance.

From the time they meet,
You've eyeballed them from head to feet.

Sayin':
"She thinks she's all that."
Not even knowing how that woman views herself.
She may be busy or in a hurry,
Or her mind is some place else.

She might be quiet or just shy;
And you've already excluded her from a basic conversation,
Thinking that she turned her nose up at you;
Not even knowing she was about to ask,
"Girl, where did you get those cute shoes?"

You'll never know unless you ask
What's on a person's mind.
How about taking that into consideration,
THE NEXT TIME!

You criticize another Sista;
(Verbally or not)
That you don't know.
It just takes a second to say, "Hello"

The Brotha's Do It!

They don't have to know each other
Personally before they speak,
Throw a what's up nod or give a pound.
Just from their first meeting,
A new homeboy they have found.

Does this behavior go back to slavery?
From field hand, to house help conflict,
Have we been programmed to act this way?
It's 2004,
Is it not a new day?

We need, to embrace and uplift our fellowman
Instead of a frown,
Offer a smile to your Sista or Brotha;
And stop all the senseless killing of one another.
(Mentally and physically)

If this is not how we really want it to be;
We need to pull together and not repeat history.

Daddy Where Were You?

You said you were coming to get us this weekend,
I'd been looking forward to it all week.
But when your car never pulled into the driveway,
I couldn't eat or sleep.

To think that My daddy would lie.
I did everything I could not to cry.

Because this was the daddy of all daddy's.
He would put ice cream in our oatmeal.
So the thought of him just being a "no show"
Was too unreal.

Then I wondered;
If his new wife made last minute plans they had to attend to.
However, you can't make anyone do something they don't
want to do.

Beside, it doesn't take but a second to make a phone call
And say;
(I'm sorry, I won't be able to make it there today.)
But instead, you wait a few days.

You called with some story about an excursion you were going
on.
Later surprised to find out,
When we called you back
You were still at home.

What possibly can you say to this?
NOTHING!
Just try keeping up that lie on our next visit.

Now the tears of disappointment that were never shed
The day you didn't come through,
Turned into unspoken bitterness and anger towards you.

What is a child to do,
When the words can't be expressed,
Because on a pedestal they held you?

He Said, "I Do"
But His Actions Says, "I Don't"

Why must you have an attitude with me?
When it's your man
That's not where he's supposed to be,
Focus your anger towards him, not me!

After all, I'm not the one in the relationship with you.
Don't fault me for him
Wanting' to have his cake and eatin' it too.

Don't call my number that you got from his cell phone.
Talk to him when he gets home.

You don't have papers on me,
And by the looks of it;
Barely on that so-called man.
You got what you thought was a man, but mentally a boy,
Now you want to make him into a husband.

He wasn't ready in so many ways
And you knew that was the case.
But you didn't wait for God to complete him.
So, after him you continued to chase.

If a man tells you
He's not ready to settle down,
Coming in late and acting strange;
Don't fool yourself to think that just because he said,
"I Do";
After the honeymoon his habits will change.

In Every Situation Lies a Positive: A Purpose, And a Message See It, Learn It, Grow from It.

With an unknown destination, clouds move in the sky.
When things happen in life; human nature's response is:
How? What? And Why?

In everything God has a plan.
Without spiritual guidance, unexplainable situations
You wouldn't understand.

Grace, Mercy, Knowledge, Wisdom, Protection and Guidance
Are all things that God has promised his people to refrain
From growing weary,
And making a firm decision to faint not
Through negative occurrences, good can be obtained.

But you ask,
What good can come from a child playing outside
Being killed in the crossfire's of a drive by?

I even wonder why it was time for MY daddy to die!

What good comes from the ones who remain;
The day those men demolished the
World Trade Center
With a hijacked airplane?

What positive comes to the boy who is repeatedly raped
By his mother's boyfriend?
Too afraid to tell her,
But when he does,
The blame is placed on him for not coming to her sooner.
Now she's serving a life sentence in the State Penn.

Why, do people sell their bodies to provide?
Some are earning more than being on a 9 to 5.
Seeking out help from the church;
Just to be shunned by those who
Act as though they've been saved all of their lives.

What's positive in that?

You want to understand.
In every situation, there's a Message and a Lesson.
It's up to you to See it – Learn it – and Grow from it;
In order not to repeat the process again.

If you think about the positive that came from the sufferings
Jesus went through,
Things that a regular man could never endure.
Looking back on his struggles to save you and me.
How many people do you know
That would lay down their lives for us to live in eternity?

Something indeed can come from a negative path.
Things that go in an unexplained direction,
Do not always turn out bad.

Blood On The Highway

Why must you speed up behind me?
(You're thinking)
You're not able to drive any faster than the car in front of you
Will allow you too.
Still, they act all irate while flashing up their middle finger at you;
When you look at them in your rear view.

So they bob and weave in and out of traffic
To frustrate themselves even further
Because other lanes are at a standstill.
Instead of throwing their hands up,
They might want to keep a grip on their steering wheel.

Out of sight they go for about a mile or two.
Oops!
Spoke too soon,
Cause there you are again
Looking' into your mirror
With them staring back at you.

On your bumper again they ride.
Now you slow down, to pull off to the side.

Evidently, they're in a hurry
And you want them to get where they need to be
So much anger in their eyes as they proceed to pass, you can see.

While looking at their expression, but not really knowing what to do,
When they pulled out a gun attempting to shoot at you.

So taken aback,
Not looking in the back
To notice how your cousin started to bleed.
How did all this occur when you were just going to get something to eat,
Right up the street?

You never know what's on a person's mind
Or what they may be going through.
Think of this fictional scenario the next time a car is tailing you.

Back In Tha Day

If what the world needs now is love, sweet love;
(They say)
It's the only thing that there's just too little of.
Then we really need help and guidance from above.
Because I can think of other things there's too little of.

Like, self- respect, trust, honesty, happiness,
The list goes on.
If the children are our future,
What will they know
If they're not being taught anything at home?

-Do We Have a Future?-

It seems as though everyone is angry these days;
With limited kind words to say.

What happened to the good ole days?

Back in tha day,
We would make up games
And play them in the street.
We ran races with bare feet, while feeling the heat of the concrete.

Everyone now is out for self.
Mentality of:
(What's yours is mine, and what's mine is mine.)

Gone are the times when you did wrong
When your mama wasn't home,
Then, your friend's mama would spank your behind.
Nowadays, that's even a crime.

When did we take this wrong turn?
There's a lot still we could stand to learn.

The legal system is claiming our black men;
So much disrespect for young women,
Being constantly called out of the birth name they were given.

They're also women doing a good job of disrespecting themselves in videos,
Wearing nothing more than two strands of dental floss.
(It seems).
While the men at least have on a wife beater T-shirt and a pair of jeans.

What do our kids have to look forward too,
If these are the things we continue to do.

If this is considered Generation X,
THEN
What will become of the next?

God Bless America
(Blessed or Greed)

Why should God bless America?

The meaning of Blessed is:
Empowered to prosper.

Is America not running over with prosperity?
I mean,
The cup of prosperity has runneth over for us.
And surely, Goodness and Mercy has followed us –
In our days, on this earth.

It's true that some may not be
(Materially)
Well to do as others,
But we are still,
Blessed!

Periodically, we must all endure
The storms of life;
But we are blessed to be able to get back up again.

Look around!
Does America not have electronic abilities, luxuries, and opportunities
That is not afforded to other countries?
And we still have our hands out for more.

Blessed or Greed?

It's unfortunate that tragedy on 9/11 occurred.
It's a shame that such a tragedy transpired
In order for some people to come together and pray.
People who ordinarily wouldn't give each other the time of day.

On the other hand, there are those who have walked around
Disregarding the whole situation.
Just look at the
Nightly News or at CNN
And you'll see that we are indeed a blessed nation.

Those carrying on (business as usual) because,
They were not directly affected by it.
To them I say, please take heed of the signs and warnings.
The greater the denial, the greater the tragedy;
And it's still not over yet.

A lot of things go on in our so-called "Great America;"
That we never hear or see.
And you think America is such a great place to be.

But you still say, God bless America?
He has been blessing America!

We all need to take personal inventory
Of what we have come through thus far.
Instead of just existing
And walking around with blinded eyes,
We need to recognize how blessed we really are.

Rather than running around with your flags
And logos of God Bless America;
Some of that time should be spent,

Asking God what he might require of you.
Then focus on doing your best to repent.

I have to say,
God has been so good to me,
That if He doesn't bless me anymore than he already has,
I say,
" God I bless your name".

C. L. Givens

Drama On the Job

You get to work
And someone has an attitude with you.
You don't know why, and could care less.
You're just there to do your job
And for others there's no need to impress.

They get upset if any little thing is left undone on the prior shift.
To do anything more than what is asked of them
A finger they won't lift.

But they're always pointing that finger at you.
About something you may have forgotten to do.

All of the while,
Holding inside whatever the problem may be.
You're greeted in the morning with an angry "Hello"
And sort of a grunt when they leave.

Rolling of the eyes starts when they come to work the next day.
Whatever the issue is,
They still don't bother to say.

While they listen to negativity from others lips
And this mess they harbor in their heart.
Why should you let it bother you,
Let them tear themselves apart.

So just keep coming to work,
Doing your job and be as professional as you can.
Continue to add them daily in your prayers
And possibly one day you could become friends again.

Anyhow

Regardless of the circumstances
And even in your lack of finance
You need to
(Rejoice) ANYHOW!

When the very person you thought would always remain true
And seemed to understand all you were going through,
Now is no longer there for you,
You need to
(Love) ANYHOW!

When your child support check is late coming to you
And T.U. Electric says,
"Ma am we're sorry, there's nothing we can do"
While lighting candles to see that night; yet and still;
You need to
(Pray) ANYHOW!

When you get evicted from your dream home
And when going out to your car to pick your kids up from school
And it's gone,
You need to
(Praise God) ANYHOW!

These tests and trials come only to make you strong.
God is walking with you and ordering your steps
Even if you feel you're all alone.

I wouldn't trade my storms in this life for anything, you see.
Everything I have gone through is what makes me,
ME.

Although, thru this journey;
If I knew then, what I know now,
No matter what you think or say,
I'm gonna
(Thank) Him ANYHOW!

Love (Reflection)

Love? Or Is It?

I've often wondered why love has to be such a chore.
As soon as he steps out of your boundaries
You're ready for him to walk out of your door.

People say it requires much work
And sometimes you might want to scream.
But for the right person,
OH WHAT JOY IT BRINGS.

Some think that buying gifts for their partner will make them happy,
And though it may seem.
At some point you should realize
That true love doesn't cost a thing.

Loving someone is hard,
If they don't let you.
No matter what you say, try, or do.

Maybe love is like being addicted
To a mind-altering drug,
Or maybe you should make better mate choices,
Instead of the neighborhood thug.

Sometimes your perception of that person
Is what you want them to be.
If the truth is told, they don't have a problem with themselves,
Who they are, is what you see.

Don't get into the mindset
That you don't deserve better than that.
Once you know your worth,
You'll know that's not the fact.

You have to live and learn from life's lessons
That is presented to you.

Keep your head up and don't turn back
And only to yourself stay true.

I know it may sound simple on paper,
But to overcome the cycle is a process.
If you want to make better choices for yourself,
This is one thing that's crucial to your success.

Caterpillar to Butterfly

If you always judge a book by its cover, you may never discover,
Why certain people are predestined to enter into your life.
You've totally excluded them from friendship status because they didn't appear to be your "type".

Allowing the minds excessive roaming to take you too far.
Opposed to exploring new possibilities by shutting the door to your heart.

Oblivious to the fact that this woman
Could have been a beneficial asset to you.
Because she didn't look or act exactly like you would have wanted her to.

She may have been a "diamond in the rough,"
Or a "caterpillar that is not yet a butterfly."
Not patient enough for the metamorphosis to occur, nor having the desire to try.

With her wings fully bloomed: powerful, strong, & displaying colors beautifully bright.
She's developed into who she was placed on earth to be, now traveling in full flight.

Coasting through life's lessons learned, this butterfly has flown away.
She has fulfilled her purpose, and there's no reason to stay.

Anticipating for what lies ahead, this butterfly is long gone.
Unlimited wind beneath her wings as she's carried with intensity into another zone.

Taking with her the knowledge of something that to YOU was unknown.
That this experience was your test, and in the caterpillar phase, you should have held on.

For she did know her purpose for being sent into your life.
But because you closed your heart and judged a book by its cover, the butterfly you let fly away was sent to be your wife.

Before turning a present away because it's not packaged just the way you like,
Consider this test, so you don't end up lonely & alone for the rest of your life.

Dedicated to the ONE that got away!

Love Poem to Myself

I'm in love with myself
No matter what anyone may think about me.
I love my brown skin and proud of my hair being nappy.
I am what you see.

I may not be the size I desire to be,
But that's not anyone's fault besides myself,
And the junk food I like to eat.

Beautiful inside and out, allow me to be me
And you be you.
It doesn't matter what name I'm called; it's what I answer to.

You may try to discourage me from my goals and dreams
And being all that I can be.
I don't want what you have, or be like you,
Because what God has for me is for me.

So as long as I'm pleasing God, while staying true to HIM
And knowing that I have nothing to prove to anyone else.
How others view me is irrelevant.
Through experience and maturing in life, I've learned to
encourage myself.

Just Because It's Dark Doesn't Mean You're In Darkness

If you ask me, I'll tell you I'm single
Even though I'm seeing someone else's man.
It works out fine for me,
Because a committed relationship, I'm not interested in.

On the outside looking at this situation
It may appear strange.
But, I don't have time to be concerned with anyone but myself,
So something otherwise I'm not trying to arrange.

The lovin is SOOO intense when he does stop by.
To teach a new dog, new tricks
Would take too much time and efforts so why try?

I'm comfortable with the way things are
Or maybe used to it or content.
Besides, I don't have many opportunities
To go out and mingle with new faces.
So with this woman's man my extra time is spent.

Why should I care, men have been doing this for years?
Sometimes leaving the other woman unaware.
Or maybe she does know, and she doesn't care.

But, as for this scenario:
This particular man's woman seemed not to be aware.

Because judging from the expression on her face,
When she caught us in THEIR bed.
Now here I lay,
On this hospital gurney with bullet fragments in my head.

(DAMN!)

I should have taken the time to get my own man.

The dirt I thought was being done in the darkness
Came to light.
Maybe I would not have gotten caught up,
If the lovin wasn't SOOO right.

I guess what goes around does come back around.
That will be remembered in my next life.

Cause as for this one [it's a rap.]

What I thought was a secret love affair had me bound.
Now, here I reside six feet under ground.

HOW, DID I, GET HERE?

C. L. Givens

The Perplexity of Love

Why does this man lie?
And why do I cry, when I don't expect anything more?
Why am I pacing the floor at a quarter past four?

Why do I wait by the phone for his call?
Why do I allow him to call at all?

Why am I on this emotional rollacoaster when it costs too much to ride?
How did I get to this point, what happened to my pride?

The longer I stay, is like I'm missing pieces of my soul.
So why is it so hard for me to let go?

Maybe it's because I can see his potential.
Or maybe I'm just mental.

Maybe I want to mother him.
While he considers it smothering him.

I know he loves me.
At least that's what he told me.
Though physically, he's never shown me.
But otherwise, why would he be here with me?

Then again, he's not here with me, he said he was going to the store.
That was earlier today, now it's a quarter past four.
Why do I allow him to make me cry, when I should have been requiring more?

I love him, and I know he needs me to survive.
I've written now until it's a quarter past five.

I don't like how he treats me, but I'm willing to stay.
Oops!! I've got to go, cause he's just pulled into the driveway.

WHY?

This has been the journaling thoughts of a woman warring in her mind
Of why she stays in a disfuctional relationship. She feels that she's all he has although it compromises her self worth and happiness.
(She feels that she's his only hope of stability.)

Written by
C.L. Givens

Love and Lies

I'm tired of crying,
And I'm sick of you lying,
[Especially about little stuff.]
No longer will I remain in this one sided relationship.
I'm fed up and I've had enough.

I'm going to my mamma's house,
So don't fix you're mouth,
To let another lie come out of your face.
As a matter of fact,
You should move out of my way right now,
Before we get to rearranging this place.

I've had enough of pacing the floor
And watching the door at all hours of the night.
I know I can find someone that will appreciate the woman I am
And know how to treat me right.

Even though your body's been here
Your mind has been absent for awhile.
I wanted to believe in you for the sake of the kids,
Or maybe I was in denial.

Oh, and by the way,
Just because you didn't see me,
I saw you AGAIN, with another woman at the movie.

So go ahead with Yvonne, LaShun, or Dawn,
Whomever you just finished talking to on my phone line.
Whichever one of your WOMEN it may have been this time.
Because my previous tears of sorrow are now of happiness,
And WITHOUT YOU I'LL BE JUST FINE!

C. L. Givens

Ode To A Love I Haven't Experienced Yet

I spotted you from across the crowded room working.
There was something about you,
That made me do something I wouldn't ordinarily do.

Like slipping you my number and name.
You seemed so professional,
Not someone just in your profession to meet new women.

Could it have been the confident
Aura that you exude?
Professional, yet crazy sense of humor
That drew me to something new.
Or the connection I felt in your eyes and smile
Each time I look at you.

Inspite of the age difference,
It had been a while since I met someone
That I was really interested in.
I was curious to find out more about you;
If nothing else we could at least become good friends.

I know I'm not the normal type of woman
That would physically appeal to you;
Meaning the fact that I'm not a size two.

Where men are more visual,
We woman tend to lean more towards
Personality and mental.

Often times the thought comes to mind,
Would things be any different
Had we crossed that friendship line
The night you came to have dinner with me?
But I can't dwell on passed events or
Coulda, woulda, or should be.

I can only look forward to what the future holds.
God only knows.
I just have to wait and see.
Eventhough I wouldn't object
If circumstances changed
By the time you turned thirty.

Friends, To Lovers, To Nothing!

For twelve years we were best friends,
But then we crossed that line.
Opening myself up to the unknown,
I figured maybe it was about that time.

It was actually good for about two years,
Starting wonderfully, now being more than just friends.
Slowly I felt you pulling your emotions away,
Which was the beginning of the end.

YOU DID THE BATE AND SWITCH!

You batted me into something I thought I needed at that time,
And then you pulled the switch.
After I opened my heart to love,
You threw me a curved pitch.

So we tried going back to being just friends,
But that wouldn't ever be the same again.
We then tried to remain doing the hook'n up thang.

I WANTED MORE.
YOU DIDN'T.
SO BE GONE!
YOU WOULDN'T.
You still frequent my home.
I had to let go,{partially}

My mind knew for sanity purposes
That we had to go our separate ways.
But my heart didn't want to follow suit,
Reminiscing on the good OLE days.

For a while, back and forth we went,
{until}
I couldn't take it anymore,
That emotional roller coaster had me spent,
{I had to get off.}

I had to come to grips with the friendship we once had no longer could be.
Especially on that winter night
When you called me;
To say, your ex-girlfriend was pregnant by you.
I thought maybe I heard that wrong,
Because surely this could not be true.

While saying to myself,
{Self, ain't this some SHIT-,
When I thought I was the ONLY ONE,
This man was having a relationship with.}

Everything is not always what you think it is.
Now drowning my sorrow with wine and tears.
Sitting here back at square one.
I HAVE WASTED SO MANY YEARS!

Look a the red flags that you do see,
And listen to what is not verbally said.
Maybe you won't end up like me.
Pacing the floor and fighting mad.

C. L. Givens

The Day I Died

If you love me like you say you do,
Why must you keep putting your hands on me,
And tightly gripping my arm?
Cause the hand I just felt across my face
Didn't feel like a hand of love, but of harm.

The love that I thought I knew
Doesn't sting like this or hurt physically.
Love shouldn't come with bruises
Visibly seen on me.

But you have bruised me in ways
That I can't verbally express at all.
You have bruised my spirit
And tarnished my soul.

When I gave up everything for you.
I gave up my kids, and contact with my family.
Most importantly, I lost love for myself,
And I've been out of touch with reality.

But you love me?
Right?
So were have you been all night?

While continually mistreating me the way you do,
You tell me repeatedly that no one will ever WANT me but you.

If this is being WANTED,
Then I may as well go ahead and
Die Right Now!
But Wait!
I'm already dead,
[Walking dead that is.]

Minimized to just an empty frame.
I can't bear to face myself in the mirror;
I'm too ashamed.
And still, after all that you've put me through,
With what is left of me,
"I Love You."
But,
"I Hate You"
For the person I've allowed myself to turn into.
And yet, I cannot muster up enough strength to walk away
from you.

I would give anything
To be able to love myself again
And walk out of this room with
No doors or walls.
Instead of being imprisoned in my own mind
And continually giving you my all.

I Need Some One By My Side. Or Do I?

Am I lonely or just tired of being alone?

Do I really want a lifetime companion,
Or just have someone to call in despair?
Or do I want someone
No matter how good or bad things get who's always there?

Or when someone gets too close to me,
Do I subconsciously push him away?
So my wall can remain up,
My vulnerable side not seen,
Being complacent in my selfish ways.

Not wanting to compromise,
And seeing things through my own eyes.

Just viewing things how I would like for them to be.
But then again,
It would take a special person
To put up with someone like me.

I don't know if I'll ever be married,
Have another long-term relationship,
Or happy with being single and free.

I do know that I won't have another relationship
Were I'm so consumed with him,
That in the process, I loose me.

Know Your Self First

As women do we really know what we want?
Do we prefer a certain type of guy?
Or if he has half of our requirements do we attempt to try?

Can we overlook the fact that instead of water waves, his hair is really nappy?
Or that he's not driving what he told you he was, [in fact his car is really crappy?]

Can we pretend that it doesn't matter that he still resides at his mamma house?
Or when you've gone on dates, he rarely takes his wallet out?

For some, problems arise with the physical.
He shows up favoring'"Big Ruben," when he said he favored "Tyrese."
Or that those jeans he has on looks like he got them from the dirty clothes instead of neatly creased.

Whatever happened to compatible conversation, goals, aspirations, and a personality?
Now it's all about "what you look like," "what you're driving," and "what can you do for me!"

Know yourself first, and what YOU have to bring to the table.
And don't discredit a man for his "ain't got's" cause one day he may be able.

Able to live in his potential and do all he sets out to do.
Know what it is you really want, instead of settling for who wants you.

Who's Deceiving Whom?

You say I've got you
Even if it's wrong or right,
Even only for one night.

This is about a woman seeing an attached man.
She's trying to pull every trick from her hat
To make him more than a friend.
To unimaginable lengths she's willing to bend.

She desperately wants to make him her own.
1.Looking up how to cast a love spell.
2.Also, sleeping with his drawers under her pillow.
3.And, even calling the Psychic Network on the phone.

Now she's come up with the notion,
Of mixing together a little love potion.

She's thinking:
[You'll be mine before the night is through.]
Dreaming of the day they will be at the altar
Exchanging there I DO'S.

POSESSIVENESS
CONTROLISM
INSANITY
All of which are emotions going through this union of infidelity.

The things some will do for
LOVE, LUST, INFATUATION,
Or however you would like to label it.
She'll do anything she can fathom
To make this affair permanent.

He comes by after work,
But never spends the night.
She hears him whispering on his cell phone telling his wife
He's working late tonight.

They have to savoir every moment,
Because it won't be long,
Before he has to go home.
Public appearances are off limits
Because he is well known.
He fears being busted, nowadays
With everyone carrying around these camera phones.

He tells her he loves her,
However he's not unhappy with his wife.
He just enjoys a little extra curricular activity on the side,
And grateful that she's willing to oblige.

While smiling in agreement,
Because he DOES know the right things to say and do,
Doesn't keep her from longing to be in his wife's shoes.

Smiling in his face
And conjuring up remedies of love behind his back; as she thinks
{He'll finely be mine or I'm Gonna Die Try'n.}

Maybe if she could have his baby
It'll keep him around.
Dreaming of trips to the mall
And then to the playground.

Then they could go to Lamaze class together,
Basketball practice and football games.
Praying that one of those remedies will actually work soon
And she'll be the one that's wearing his last name.

She calls her girlfriends to tell them how much she hates him
And wishes he would die
And how nightly she hugs her pillow tight and cries.
Time after time.

But all of that emotional drama ceases
When the doorbell rings.
Cause soon she'll be skinning and grinning
Like she's the one wearing his ring.

And all of what she has to go through,
Just to see him for an hour or two,
Doesn't even come to mind.

After all, this brother is finer than cat hair,
With teeth that sparkle and shine bright white
Like he's a rep. for crest.
Skin smooth and chocolate
From his size 14 shoe to that lightly hairy chest.

Him being oblivious to what's on her mind,
As she seems all bubbly with glee.
Being blinded by lust,
He's unaware of how devious she can really be.

Not knowing that what she's really thinking is:
{Oh yeah, brotha, keep drinking that wine.
One day you will be mine, or I'm Gonna Die Try'n}

Break the Cycle

What is this web of deceit you've entwined yourself in?

Repeating the cycle that the one before you did.
Cycle of shame and untruths you witnessed as a kid.

The same one you speak ill of.
The same one you'd sworn never to be an example of.
She being that same one, of whom you're a product of.

You; being a product of a web of deception adultery, and dishonesty,
Should thrive to be stronger than your generation before you could be.

Develop that strength to pass to your offspring's.
Wanting for them to grow up witnessing positive things.

If your companion has another committed attachment,
Courtship involving you and he is not meant.

Dissension in his household he tries to explain.
Have wisdom to know that he's telling another the same.

Allow him to cut ties with his wife,
Before you become equated into his life.

Decide in your mind,
If you really want to tolerate being placed on the sideline.

Reality of your self-worth must be unknown.
Because you've not gotten the courage to move on.

Maybe it's true when they say, "the apple doesn't fall too far from the tree".

Regardless of the distance fallen, it's not necessary to replicate deceptive activity.

Picking Up The Pieces Of A Shattered Heart

I love you so much that it hurts.
It hurts that I poor my all into you,
But you don't put forth effort to make this work.

I love you with my soul.
I've loved you since I was 18 years old.

It's more of a spiritual love.
One that there's no definition of.

Thinking back on the times that I needed you most,
You used to be there.
A soft place to fall when no one else seemed to care.

When I was sick taking care of me is what you would do.
In reminiscing on the good times,
That's one of the things I loved about you.

How just for no reason,
You'd come over to cook for us.
Even when you were without transportation
And had to ride the bus.

Being in your presents used to be enough.
That's why I don't understand
This distance developing between us.

The laughter we once shared is now gone.
Conversations ending
With me slamming down the phone.

I've tried and tried to rid my system of you,
Which is hard even after all we've been through.

Sometimes I would get so mad at you.
Looking back now I see,
The things that would frustrate me the most
Were the issues I myself struggle with daily.

With so much unspoken anger,
Can we find the love or is this the end?
Maybe in another lifetime,
We may be able to try again.

I will move on but it will take time,
Because when I meet someone new,
The comparison of you still comes to mind.

I've come to grips with the type of relationship
We once shared will be no more.
This became apparent to me
The last time I watched you walk out my door.

Reflection in Solitude

Suddenly I've discovered this unfamiliar world of the unknown.
Caught between the realization that things weren't going to change,
And not wanting to move on.

When I should have been long gone,
Contentment kept me holding on.

Now faced with being on my own,
But not finding solace in being alone.

In passed times always having someone to call my own,
I sit here now in solitude reminiscing on a love I'd once known.

Trying to figure out what went wrong,
Acknowledging there may have been truth in me being too headstrong.

With my thoughts driven into reflection,
Maybe I could have shown more compassion and affection.

Before the next relationship I decide to embark upon,
I must undergo reconstruction, so that I don't continue on this path of self- destruction.

The most profound discovery of this reflective journey that I've been on,
Was that you never were the man that I thought I had known.

Now two Christmas's have come and gone.
When will I REALLY decide to move on?

Continually pressing rewind,
And being held captive in my mind.

[For how long?]

That's the million-dollar question,
But the answer is still unknown.

UNSATISFIED

What you thought was a nice layout,
(But knowing in the back of your mind)
It would compromise your worth.
Later on to discover, it was planted on artificial turf.

You thought the grass would be greener,
But after time you found her to be meaner.

Meaner than I ever was.
Mistaking infatuation
For what you wanted to be love.

With your nose wide open and eyes wide shut,
What you thought was bright in color and new,
Would end up making a fool of you!

Stuck in complacency,
Now as the grass has begun to wither.
Where there once was a house of warmth and happiness,
Has become cold and bitter.

NOW YOU WANT ME TO RECONSIDER!

A Wedding Without A Marriage

You're at the altar exchanging your vows,
As you look to notice faces in the crowd.
Everyone who's anyone has come to attend this ceremony.
All of the while you know for yourself
That this show that you are putting on is phony,

You've spent all of the money you had.
Desperately trying to please your mom and dad.

At the reception you're socializing, reminiscing, and laughing
With people (some wishing that they were in your shoes,)
Unaware of the truth of what you're really going through.

Oblivious to the fact that, after the last dance is danced
And you prepare to leave,
That HUSBAND of yours will be hitting the streets.

And how those candles that were just used for decorations,
You HAVE to take them home,
Because your electricity is no longer on.

Your bill money was spent
On a big wedding,
That was not going to be a marriage from the beginning.
But you wanted to be married SO bad
Now look at the predicament you're in.

He's never at home
And you call all around town to see if anyone has seen him.
When you should be devising a plan
Of how and when to leave him.

I don't know why you bother,
Because when he is at home,
He doesn't bother to talk to you.
When he does,
He's yelling about something you did or didn't do.
By his side you firmly stand.
You've isolated yourself from your family and best friend.

When are you going to realize,
That EVERYONE can't be lying about your man?
Why must you think "they're just jealous"
Because they don't have anyone and they don't understand?

Who would want a mate that bad
To go through all of the things that yours puts you through?
Oh yeah, I forgot,
No one knows the real him but YOU!

Calling me,
Because you know I'll be there to listen to you
After the yelling ceases and he's given you the blues.

Ok, See, what I would do is....
No wait, never mind, you won't listen,
You never do.
If you did you wouldn't have said "I DO!"

Now in a mess,
When it was your family
And their friends you wanted to impress.

So I'll keep praying that GOD changes your mind,
And pray that you don't wind,
Up in a casket when he looses his temper the next time.

Truthfully, I don't want to be,
The one who writes a poem for your Eulogy.

UNTITLED

I set my pen in motion
To see if there is one ocean,
That we can sail.

What course?
What charter?
Do we dare face these raging waters
That engulfs so many?
Who sat out to sail a peaceful course:
But wound up in a sea of indifference and despair.

Who can calm the changing tide?
Who can make us look inside?
Our own changing lives?

Water: like love, ebbs and flows,
Can we contain a level course, and reach a safe haven?
Or must we be like the Raven?
Never more?

If rain falls into each life:
Cannot we control the droplets that define our own being?
Do we tread the waters, seeking and being blind by our own seeing?
Can we prevail?
Can we set sail?
Can we not drown in our sense of CONNECTION?
Can we set course
In the same direction?

I tried again today, not to LOVE YOU
But once again, as always before,
My heart overruled my arrogance,
And once more
Changed the direction of our plight.

C. L. Givens

Check yourself; my horoscope read,
Can you invite some one in, or has your soul become dead??
To new ideas,
To new dreams,
You can't be right all the time -IT SEEMS!

Inspired by Leslie Givens - Aug.2000

DECEPTION

Where have you been?
You were supposed to pick me up from work,
But I had to call a friend.

When I saw you,
You gave me excuse after excuse about your whereabouts
And what you had been through.

I looked into your eyes,
And saw what you were saying were all lies.

Even before now,
The statements you made I found to be untrue.
I'm thinking right about now, I've had enough of you.

Thoughts of infidelity did come to mind.
But were soon erased
When you assured me that everything was fine.

Overtime the disappearing acts became greater.
You started staying out later and later.

Even with the crying and apologizing
I read right between the lines.
My intuition was indeed correct;
There WAS someone else this time.

There was another love
You were giving your money to.
Her name was CRACK COCCAINE
And she had a hold on you.

Because you said you wanted to change,
Against my better judgement I decided to stick by your side.
Later to find that, that was another one of your lies.
That was a strong- hold I was not able to compete with or dare try.

Now you're at the point were you will do or say anything for her,
(Just to get another hit!)
This lifestyle I'm not accustomed to,
And I'M NOT WILLING TO GET USED TO IT.

Seek Help!
Look inward for the answers
Instead of placing the blame of your life long
Issues on everyone else.

I'm glad I followed my intuition instead of my heart,
Before your deception continued to tare me apart.

Comforted in the fact that now I know the truth,
To think, I was just about to marry You.

I do wish you well,
Eventhough you made my life a living HELL!

No longer will I sing the "WHERE HAVE YOU BEEN" blues,
I pray that oneday I don't turn on my TV
And see you on the evening news.

SOUL MATES

I knew when I first met you; you and I were predestined to be.
Eventhough you were dating someone then,
That didn't mean much to me.

You wanted to just be friends
And I did to.
But when you knew I was spending time with others
It became a problem for you.

In spite of that, I went on with my life
However thoughts of you did come to mind.
Regardless of the current situation,
I felt we would be together in a matter of time.

After a while, we became exclusive and at first things were o.k.
Until you wanted to run around with your friends and
continually stayed out late.

Now that grew to be a problem for me,
Because at home is where I wanted you to be.

At that time I didn't realize that I was subconsciously pushing
you out of the door.
Sharing little of myself, but from you requiring more and
more.

In my mind, as long as I did the things around the house like
I needed to,
Everything would be fine between me and you.

I guess I was wrong,
Cause when I looked up, you were gone.

How could you leave me?
Especially now, since we have this new baby!

I was doing what I thought was pleasing you.
I couldn't see that I was operating out of my own selfishness.
When I thought I was putting your needs before mine,
Instead I ended up loosing myself in the process.

Although bitter I know,
This separation was necessary in order for me to grow.

Self-evaluation had to take place in order for me to know that
Another person could not complete me.
With God's guidance,
I had to become the woman I was placed here to be.

Through our struggles and back and forth's,
For us to now become good friends
Reassures me that it's never to late.
I still believe in my heart
You are and forever will be my SOUL MATE.

Why Do I Keep Loving Someone Who Doesn't Love Me?

Have you ever been in a relationship where you lost yourself to please him?
No matter what you did or said was ever good enough for him.

Because he already told you from the beginning he wanted to just be friends.
You assumed with all the attention you were showing him, he would soon give in.

Wanting so desperately for him to be the ONE for you,
Cause he shares similar interests, morality, and goals as you do.

Not to mention, you're tiring of searching for a stepfather for your kids.
You felt when you met this man your searching came to an end.

End of the lonely days and single nights.
If only he could love you like you'd like.

With unspoken communication, you knew you and he were now more than friends.
Finding reassurance with the additional times together you would spend.

But never verbally discussing if his feelings were still the same.
You took the frequent visits spent to mean that things had changed.

Or maybe blinded by what you wanted to see,
Or how you wanted this relationship to be.

So out of the kindness of your heart, you wanted to surprise him with a picnic of his favorite things.
But the SURPRISE was on you, when he greeted you at the door half-dressed and rushing you to leave.
While catching a glimpse of his companion of choice for this eve,
You're shocked, stunned, and upset by the entire scene.
Your mind starts racing as you think,
"He chose her over me!"

Processing the night's events as you speedily drive home.
Trying to fight back the tears as your comforted by your girls on the phone.
Saying how much of a dog he is, and how he lead you on, and in the same breath asking, [what could have gone wrong?]

Maybe because after the first date, you made it your mission,
To persuade him into playing more than the "friend" position.

And so you thought if you wooed him and whined and dinned,
He would see things your way in a matter of time.

Wanting to know where the wires got crossed so you can resolve this issue.
Pleading to communicate now with no luck, because he has a restraining order against you.

He saw you on more than one occasion stalking him from
across the street,
When you thought you were being careful and discreet.

Opening your self to a person that made it clear what he
wanted from the start.
Now emotionally drained, with him unaware that he's tugging
at the strings to your heart.

For answers, you continually still are demanding.
Was It All For Love, or A Big Misunderstanding?

Part 2: The Answer
From a Man's Perspective

Why Do I Keep Loving Someone Who Doesn't Love Me?

I wished I could have loved you but first I need to love me.
When I told you from the start that only your friend is what I wanted to be.

I wanted your companionship
Without having a committed relationship.

I'm sorry you thought I led you on.
To me we were just hanging out and having fun.

I do appreciate all the things you did and the places we would go.
You said you wanted to take me out and buy me things and I wasn't about to say "no".

In my eyes friendship was all that it was,
The extra added benefits were always a plus.

I do care about you and frequent thoughts of you may come to mind,
But committing to one person is not something that I desire for myself at this time.

Maybe the wires got crossed on your line, cause I stated my intent.
I enjoyed your company that's why a lot of time with you I spent.

You say I should have told you I was seeing someone else, but to me it wasn't a big issue.
I never interrogate you about your whereabouts whenever I'm not with you.

How could "just friends" mean something totally different to you and me?
Or is it that your judgement was clouded by how you wanted us to be?

I thought we had the same non-verbal understanding.
Apparently not, because here on my porch you're standing,
In pouring down rain yelling, screaming, and ranting.
For some kind of explanation you are demanding.

In this rage is a side of you I never new.
I don't know what other explanation I can offer you.

I apologize for not being able to tell you what you want to hear.
But I thought I made my intentions very clear.

Maybe befriending you was a mistake on my part.
Hostility is something I try to avoid,
Especially when I never new I was breaking your heart.

Before your emotions became factored into the equation,
There should have been an open line of communication.

When you felt the dynamics of this friendship starting to change,
Instead of assuming, you should have asked if I felt the same.

Please forgive me for not sharing these same feelings, though I wish I could.
Not placing the blame on anyone, but my friendship to you was extremely misunderstood!

ETERNITY
(Final Destination)

DESCIPTION OF MISSING YOU

I wrote this poem while trying to process the sudden passing of my father.

I had just spoke with him on the phone,
And just that quick, he was gone.
Always saying I LOVE YOU, is what he would end our conversations with.
But I was unaware that this would be the last time I would hear him say it.
Holding on to my faith that one day I will see him again,
I keep in my mind what the scripture says in 1THES.4: 13,14.

C. L. Givens

Missing You

Words can't express the way I feel
To sit and think about my father
Not being here is so surreal.

Just that Thursday night
I spoke with him on the phone.
Telling him that on Sunday after church,
We would be visiting him at his home.

Not even contemplating
That just a few short hours earlier that night he would be gone.

Gone to be with Jesus in the sky.
In knowing what kind of person he was,
He will be missed, so go ahead and cry.

For human nature that is how we deal.
But the heartbreak from grieving over a loved one
Will surely take time to heal.

Camouflaging emotions and feelings with humor
Was a characteristic of my dad.
He would always have a joke for you,
Even when HE was feeling bad.

So whether you knew him as
Champ, Cool Breeze, Tick, or Les.
When you do think of him,
Know that he is at rest.

He is no longer suffering
From his body's aches and pains.

With the love and wisdom he expressed to all,
His memory will always remain.

I MISS YOU DADDY!

In Loving Memory of
Leslie Givens

DESCIPTION OF LIVE IN TODAY, BECAUSE YOUR TOMORROW ISN'T PROMISED

I wrote this poem in memory of my cousin. When I first heard of his sudden passing, these are the words that came to mind. He was someone that every time you saw him, he would have a smile on his face. So the news of his home going took me by surprise especially since he was just a few years older than I am. I pray that you be blessed by this poem.

Live In Today, Because Your Tomorrow Isn't Promised

What's familiar is no longer acceptable.
I can no longer live in my yesterday,
But press on through my today.

Changing of my past ways,
Always mindful to give God thanks and prays
To be able to see another day.

Because the alternative is (taboo).
Unless faced with it
It's not frequently discussed out loud.
Death is a subject most people are afraid to talk about.

When you think of death you think:
Grief, Pain, Hurt and Sorrow.
When you hear of someone dying unexpectedly,
It's like they were
HERE TODAY AND GONE TOMMORROW.

When I think of death,
I think we should all take personal inventory of our lives,
Getting our houses in order,
And hearts right with God, constantly keeping in mind,
Just because you made it through today,
Tomorrow could very well be your time.

In Loving Memory of
Darren Sanders

DESCRIPTION OF I DON'T UNDERSTAND

This is a poem that I wrote while trying to gather understanding in my natural mind of how and why did my teenage cousin have to die in a road rage incident that occurred on the weekend before the tragedy of 9/11. He was simply just a passenger on his way home from a football game. I pray that you be blessed by this, and any other poem you may read in this book.

I Don't Understand

To the natural eye
I DON'T UNDERSTAND why
This happened the way it did.
Jeremy was mild mannered,
But yet and still a respectable kid.

Through the tears and the pain
The events of this tragedy are trying to be sorted out.
But through my faith in God,
I believe changes in some people lives will come about.

Although, I DON'T UNDERSTAND
I know it will take time to heal.
For I do know that even the strongest of people
Have endured great ordeals.

Though things happen like this everyday.
Some you never hear about;
It's considered [just another life lost.]
For eyes and hearts to be opened,
An innocent passenger had to pay the cost.

And then, you're thinking
[There are so many kids in this world out deliberately doing wrong
And deserve for their lives to come to an end.]

But if it had happened to someone deserving,
You never would have heard about it,
And you wouldn't have had this chance to look within,

Yourself to see,
How you can change your view towards life,
Because tomorrow is not promised to you or to me.

To whoever has read about this in the paper,
Or seen it on TV, there hearts go out to the family
And maybe one day we can see
How this negative situation will have some sort of positive effect.
The when, where, or how,
I DON'T UNDERSTAND
As of yet.

Although the positive in this
Will come differently to each and everyone,
The love of Jeremy
And his spirit will forever live on.

I'm a believer that everything
In this life happens for a reason.
Whether good or bad, happy or sad,
When that is determined for you
Will be in your due season.

What could you possibly say to a parent
That has lost their only son?
[Nothing]
There's nothing you can say!
Just show them you care,
And be there when they need someone to listen
And constantly keep them in your prayers.

Because none of your encouraging words,
Or your relating stories will bring them back.

Pray for their strength
And understanding and will to live on,
Even when the dearest person
In their lives are gone.

For me, personally,
I didn't even know I owned as many tears
That I have shed this week.
That's why I had to put my thoughts on paper,
Just thinking about it is hard enough,
Sometimes it's hard to speak.

So go ahead and cry, for human nature that's how we deal.
Through the sadness and tears,
You will at some point heal.

I might not understand, why this happened,
Maybe it's not for me to understand,
I am glad though he is out of this unkind world
And that he didn't have to suffer,
But I also know that grieving won't bring him back again.

We as the family
And friends need to see how,
We can learn from this experience
And move forward from now.

I know at times it's tough,
And in the heart there is still so much pain.
But please believe
That in his short time on this earth,
His leaving was not in vein.

BE BLESSED and STAY PRAYERFUL,
In Loving Memory of
Jeremy Blackshire

Description of Cycle of Life

My grandmother (my father's mother) passed away six months after he did. She was one of the people instrumental in the mends that was made in the relationship between my father and I. I wrote "Cycle of Life" in her memory.

Cycle of Life

Everything happens for a reason
And everyone is placed on this earth for a purpose
To serve in their due season.

It's amazing to me how
The Cycle of Life is orchestrated.
Meaning Life/Death

We are born; to live; to fulfill our purpose in life.
Everyone has a reason for existing;
At least that was the plan.
When our work here on earth is done,
We can return to the spirit realm again.

After our LIVING here on earth ends,
Then our eternal life with thc creator will begin.

In Loving Memory of
Claudia Givens

THE END

About the Author

C. L. Givens grew up in Plano, Texas with her mother and two sisters.

She now resides in Dallas, Texas with her two children.

She began writing in her adolescents, but actually became serious about publishing her work, when her father died unexpectedly in May of 2003. She decided she needed to look at her own "reflection" and "live, in her today because tomorrow isn't promised." No longer would she take life for granted.

And with that realization, she knew that she had to fulfill her purpose in life.

With the thoughts that God gave her, (some of which not necessarily pertaining to her), she wrote them down, and this has resulted in short stories in poetic form. Her prayer is that this book inspires and blesses each reader so that they may learn to embrace each of their "life's lessons."

Printed in the United States
47594LVS00003B/108

9 781594 08275